THE IDEAL CHRISTMAS GIFT BOOK

EDITED BY
MATT MAGUIRE

Published in 2015 by Candescent Press

Candescent Press
www.candescentpress.co.uk
info@candescentpress.co.uk

Copyright © 2015 Matt Maguire and Candescent Press.

All rights reserved. No part of this publication may be reproduced, stored in a retrieval system, or transmitted in any form or by any means, electronic, mechanical, photocopying, recording or otherwise, without the prior permission of the copyright owner.

The information in this book is vaguely accurate - but who knows these days? If you find something that you think is so wrong it makes your blood boil more than receiving a pair of socks from your best friend at Christmas, then get in touch and we'll get our top people to look into it.

Welcome to The Ideal Christmas Gift Book...

We hope you enjoy reading this book as much as we enjoyed writing it. We've tried to make sure there's something for everyone in the following pages, and we think you'll find a few of the facts truly amazing. If you're too young or too old to answer some of the quiz questions, just read the answers and then pretend you knew it all along!

And remember to give a big hug to whoever gave it to you* and also pat them (and yourself) on the back, as this copy has already earned money for charities helping those in need.

*unless it was Santa, in which case remember to leave out a thank you note for him next Christmas.

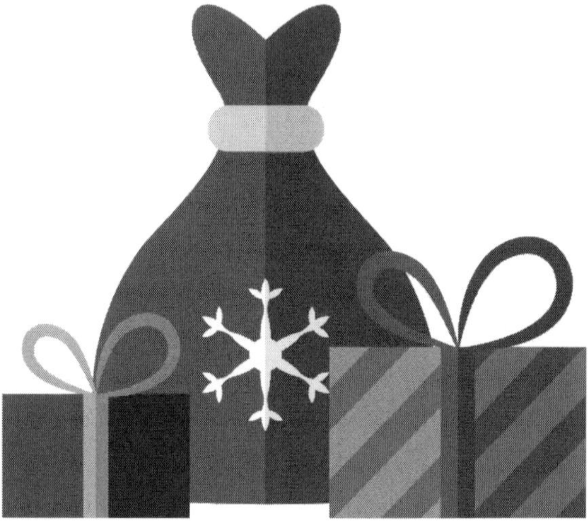

Contents

Chestnuts Joking on an Open Fire!..1

Jingling Space Bells..2

Name the Christmas Tune #1..3

It's a Festive Spot the Difference - Hooray!..4

Your 1920s Must-Have Toy!..6

Christmas at the Movies Quiz..7

Step away from the Decorations!..9

Rudolph the Red Nosed Joker..10

All Wrapped Up!..11

A Random Top 10 - Christmassy Names..12

Santa's Chinese Helpers..13

Your 1930s Must-Have Toy!..14

Twice the Magic!..15

A Quizzing We Shall Go!..17

Christmas is CANCELLED!..19

The Most Wonderful* Jokes of the Year!..20

Name the Christmas Film #1..21

The Search is on for Christmas..22

Your 1940s Must-Have Toy!..23

12 Days of Christmas for budding Scrooges!..24

You call him Santa... 30

Deck the Halls with Lots of Jokes... L-o-l-o-l O-l-o-l 31

A Random Top 10 - UK Box Office Christmas 2005 32

Christmas on the Telly Quiz 33

A Very, Very Old Card 35

Name the Christmas Tune #2 36

Your 1950s Must-Have Toy! 37

If Santa was a Jigsaw 38

Beware Krampus! 39

Feed the Elves and they will come! 40

Christmas Day People: The Quiz 41

Name the Christmas Tune #3 44

Rudolph the Bacterial Nosed Reindeer 45

Quick! Hide the Broom! 46

Your 1960s Must-Have Toy! 47

Hcrismtsa lla imdex pu 48

Hello? Hello? Is that Santa? Can I speak to an elf please? 49

How does Santa deliver all those presents in one night? 50

A Random Top 10 - Merry Christmas and a Happy New Year
in 10 languages! 51

Name the Christmas Tune #4 52

Jokin' Around the Christmas Tree 53

Your 1970s Must-Have Toy! 54

The 'Once upon a time some authors wrote about Christmas' Quiz 55

O Star of wonder, Star of night, Are you a comet or a form of planetary light?..57

The Penny Magician..58

12 Days of Wordsearch..60

Name the Christmas Film #2..61

Japan ♥ KFC @ Christmas..62

We Wish You a Joking Christmas!..63

He was (possibly not) born on Christmas Day!...............................64

Your 1980s Must-Have Toy!..65

Big Box, Little Box, Cardboard Fish?.......................................66

Eat, Drink & Be Merry: The Quiz..67

Large Swedish Goats...69

Cleverer than a Santa with two brains?.....................................70

Name the Christmas Tune #5...73

You Saw Mommy Kissing Who?!..74

Joking in the Air!..75

Who Gets Their Presents First?...76

A Random Top 10 - UK Charts Christmas 1980.................................77

Some Tree-mendous Facts..78

An Even More Random Top 10 - Some Trees....................................79

Sing-a-long-a-Christmas-quiz...80

Jingle Bells, Jingle Bells, Joking All the Way!...................................82

It's a Wonderful Wordsearch!...83

Selling Christmas...84

Your 1990s Must-Have Toy!..85

The Four Elves...86

French parents try to ban Father Christmas advert!......................88

Fun with Fruit..89

Name the Christmas Tune #6..90

Happy Birthday to the World Wide Web..91

It's Christmas Day! Here are some Answers!....................................93

    Answers - Christmas at the Movies Quiz......................................95

    Answers - A Quizzing We Shall Go!..98

    Answers - Christmas on the Telly Quiz..100

    Answers - Christmas Day People: The Quiz................................102

    Answers - The 'Once upon a time some authors wrote about Christmas' Quiz..106

    Answers - Eat, Drink & Be Merry: The Quiz.................................109

    Answers - Sing-a-long-a-Christmas-quiz.....................................111

    Answers - The Search is on for Christmas..................................114

    Answers - 12 Days of Wordsearch..115

    Answers - It's a Wonderful Wordsearch!......................................116

    Answers - Spot the difference..117

    Answers - Santa Jigsaw...118

    Answers - Hcrismtsa All Imdex Pu•..119

    Answers - Cleverer than a Santa with two brains?..................120

THE IDEAL CHRISTMAS GIFT BOOK

Chestnuts Joking on an Open Fire!

Where does Santa keep his books?

On his shELVES!

Why does Santa have a large garden?

Because he loves to Hoe Hoe Hoe!

What type of candle burns longer?

None, they all burn shorter!

Why did Santa's helper see the doctor?

He had low 'elf esteem

Jingling Space Bells

The first song performed in space was a Christmas favourite. Interesting? Maybe, but there's more to the story. On December 16th 1965 the crew of the US rocket Gemini 6 (Tom Stafford and Wally Schirra) informed Mission Control that they could see an object through the window. "We have an object, looks like a satellite going from north to south, probably in polar orbit... Looks like he might be going to re-enter soon... You just might let me pick up that thing... I see a command module and eight smaller modules in front. The pilot of the command module is wearing a red suit." Does that description sound familiar?

After a few tense moments what Mission Control heard next truly surprised them... it was the sound of a harmonica and a set of mini sleigh bells that the crew had smuggled aboard - and the song they played on them was Jingle Bells!

While we're Jingling our Bells, did you know the song wasn't originally written for Christmas? Jingle Bells was written in the 1850s by James Lord Pierpont and was to be sung at Thanksgiving.

Name the Christmas Tune #1

Breakdown of Christmas Present Desirability

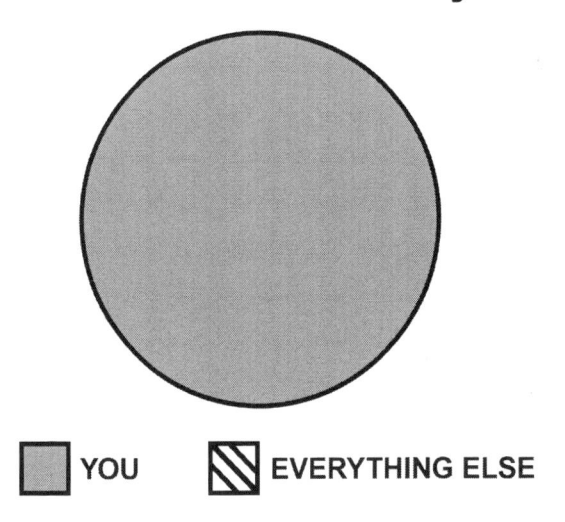

▢ YOU ◨ EVERYTHING ELSE

Find the answer at the bottom of the next page.

It's a Festive Spot the Difference - Hooray!

There are ten differences between the pictures on this page and the next - find them all, and give yourself an extra present!

Name The Tune #1: All I Want For Christmas Is You

4

While you're 'spotting', you might want to think about what's happening in the pictures, as we have no idea what's going on. A party that the gingerbread men weren't invited to? Some kind of stealth mission to steal the snowman's presents?

See page 117 for the answers.

Your 1920s Must-Have Toy!

The Yo-Yo

The earliest record we have of a yo-yo is from around 500bc in Greece, but it's possible they are even older - with many believing they were invented in China. So why was this the must-have toy in the 1920s? Well, maybe it was just time for a revival - yes, they already knew history existed in the 1920s too - or maybe it was because this was a revolutionary new design. Instead of the string being simply tied round the middle of the yo-yo, it was looped around it. This doesn't sound like much, but it meant a top yo-yoer could perform tricks that would leave the audience open-mouthed with awe!

The company that made this "round thing on a bit of string" (that's the technical term) was making 300,000 yo-yos EVERY DAY by the end of 1929, making it our 1920s must-have.

Christmas at the Movies Quiz

Film: Christmas at the Movies
Director: Santa
Date: 25th December
Cameraman: Rudolph

1. Which Christmas film has made more money at the box office than any other? How the Grinch Stole Christmas, It's a Wonderful Life, or The Polar Express?

2. What were the names of the Cop and the Cab Driver in It's a Wonderful Life? CLUE: This one is easier for Sesame Street fans.

3. What was the name of Macaulay Culkin's character in Home Alone? And for a bonus, what was the name of the 'gang' that he battled with?

4. Scrooged, with Bill Murray, is many people's favourite Christmas movie. But what book was it based on?

5. Elf is a modern Christmas Classic. Can you name the four main food groups that Elves eat?

6. The 1930s' classic, Miracle on 34th Street, was remade in 1994. Which dinosaur fan played Santa?

7. Tom Hanks stars as the Conductor in The Polar Express, but who plays Santa Claus in the movie? For a bonus point, who played Scrooge?

8. Gremlins is slightly darker than your typical Christmas movie - but it's one of our favourites! The star is the cute Mogwai called Gizmo. But what must you never do to a Mogwai after midnight, no matter how much it cries or begs? Feed it, play with it, or sing to it?

9. What is the name of the family in National Lampoon's Christmas Vacation? For a bonus who played the family's son, Rusty? CLUE: He's making a big bang as one of the highest paid TV stars of the 2010s!

10. Tim Allen stars in The Santa Clause which made a surprising amount of money at the box office. However, he co-stars in another series of movies which were even more successful - yet his face is never seen. Name the movie series and Tim's character.

See page 95 for the answers.

Step away from the Decorations!

The risk of lead poisoning from metallic Tinsel Christmas decorations was considered such a danger to children, that the US Food and Drug Administration asked companies to stop selling it. Tinsel was also once made from real silver! That proved a little expensive, and one of the most common replacements was the lead foil that led to the Americans taking action. But before you start worrying about your own decorations' lethal intentions, these days it's made of a slightly less glamorous polyvinyl chloride with a metallic coating.

While The US FDA may have helped push tinsel towards obscurity in America, it is fighting back elsewhere in the world! In a story titled "School bans killer tinsel", we read of a school banning tinsel because pupils were wearing it around their necks on the last day before the Christmas holidays.

An overreaction? Maybe, but apparently there are thousands of hospital visits around the world each year due to Christmas tree related injuries - so maybe it's best to step away from those Christmas decorations, and wrap yourself in cotton wool till January.

Rudolph the Red Nosed Joker

How do Santa's helpers learn to read?

They use the elf-a-bet

Why do Egyptian Mummies like Christmas so much?

Because of all the wrapping!

Where does Father Christmas go on holiday?

Santa Barbara

How many letters are in Santa's alphabet?

Only 25. There's No el!

All Wrapped Up!

What better time than Christmas to have some fun with wrapping paper. How about papering the door to your brother/sister/mother/father/son/daughter's bedroom? Paper quietly on Christmas Eve, with the pattern facing into their bedroom. In the morning, they'll have to burst through to reach their presents - or they might just think their present is soooo big that it's taken up the entire house!

If you've any paper left over (and always ask the paper owner's permission first), then why not paper your tree?

A Random Top 10 - Christmassy Names

DECEMBER 25

1. Holly Hunter (Oscar winning actress)

2. Klaus Heisler (the fish in the TV series American Dad)

3. Jesus Navas (a Spanish footballer)

4. Joy Adamson (Big fan of lions)

5. Gabriel Byrne (actor - The Usual Suspects)

6. Criss Angel (Magician)

7. Christian Dior (Fashion Designer)

8. (Saint) Nick Jonas (a Jonas brother)

9. Rudolph Giuliani (Politician & ex-Mayor of New York)

10. Noel Gallagher (Musician - was in Oasis)

Santa's Chinese Helpers

We all know that the people of China make a lot of stuff - and by A LOT, we mean pretty much everything. So, it won't be a surprise to find out that most Christmas decorations come from China - BUT did you know that most of them come from just one city?! Yiwu in China is even known as Christmas Village as they make more than 60% of the whole world's decorations!

If you fancy going there in person, the Christmas shop has more than 400,000 different items on sale - from glow in the dark Christmas Trees to Styrofoam snowmen. Just make sure you don't dress as an elf or you might be put to work!

Your 1930s Must-Have Toy!

Monopoly

Ah...Monopoly. We start so full of hope, rolling the dice, buying property. Then before we know it, someone has got all the cash, but won't accept your resignation. Instead they want to take all the money you have, over many, many hours. Still, if that person is you then it's brilliant isn't it?

Monopoly's origins can be traced back to just after 1900, but it really took off in the 1930s, so that's our must-have toy* of the decade. (*ok we know it's a game!)

If you're a fan of Monopoly and a fan of chocolate, then you might want to go back in a time machine to 1978, when Neiman Marcus, sold a chocolate version in their Christmas Wish Book. This wasn't just a few chocolate pieces, but an entire chocolate game - board and all. Shame it cost £400!

Twice the Magic!

Here's a really simple card trick, with a bonus – you can trick two people at once! Before you start, sort the deck into two piles, one with all the red cards and another with the black cards. Put them back together, and remember not to shuffle them.

Tell your audience that you're going to ask not just one person, but two, to pick a card, and that you'll be able to find both of them.

With the cards facing you, begin by splitting the pack in two again (red and black), then place them face down on a table.

Ask a volunteer to pick a card from the first pile. Then take the rest of the cards from them and lay them down on the table.

Repeat this for the second pile.

When both cards have been picked, ask the two 'pickers' to show their cards to the rest of the audience, so that everyone knows which cards were picked.

While they are distracted showing the cards, pick up the SECOND pile and ask the FIRST picker to replace their card anywhere in the deck.

Now pick up the FIRST pile and ask the SECOND picker to replace their card anywhere in the deck.

Place both piles face down and tell the audience you're going to identify BOTH cards picked, but first, to make things harder, you'll shuffle the cards.

Shuffle each deck individually keeping the cards face down so neither you or the audience can see the front of the cards.

Finally, combine the packs and, without further shuffling, begin to look through them - again not letting your audience see the front of the cards.

You'll easily be able to identify the cards, as the black one will be with the red cards, and the red one will be with the black cards.

Add to the show by pausing and looking at cards every now and again, and then staring at one of the pickers, so it appears that the trick is more complicated.

After a few seconds, pick out the cards and reveal them to the audience!

After the trick, make sure you take back the cards and casually shuffle them before anyone else looks at the deck.

Remember - as with any trick, practice on your own first, so that when you perform for your friends and family you'll get it right first time!

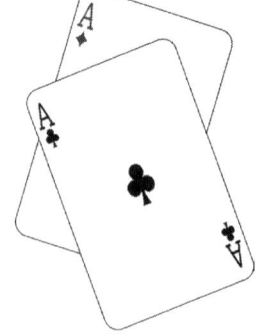

A Quizzing We Shall Go!

1. What Christmas wonder was invented by Edward Johnson and displayed at his home in New York City in 1882?

2. In Iceland, children are lucky enough to get visits from more than one gift-giving "Santa" - but how lucky are they? Do they get gifts from 3, 7 or 13 Santas?

3. During the festive period, it's traditional in many countries to kiss underneath what? Holly, Mistletoe or Eggnog?

4. If you want to write to Santa in Canada, you use the postal code HOH OHO. True or False?

5. In a 1964 movie, Santa had more than a few naughty kids to deal with. Who was Santa's foe? The Venetians, The Moon People, or The Martians?

6. Which child star said, "I stopped believing in Santa Claus when I was six. Mother took me to see him in a department store and he asked for my autograph"? Shirley Temple, Miley Cyrus or Macaulay Culkin?

Answers on page 98.

Christmas is CANCELLED!

We don't have space to explain all the complications of the English Civil War here, but we can tell you that it resulted in a ban on Christmas! The war was fought between supporters of the King and supporters of Parliament (known as Roundheads because many had very bad haircuts!). These Roundheads were led by Puritans - a group of very strict Christians, who decided that Christmas had become too big a party, and in 1647 they banned it!

It wasn't until 1660 that the ban was lifted.

The Pilgrims who went to America on the Mayflower in 1620 were also strict Puritans - so for a while Christmas was a no-no on both sides of the Atlantic!

The Most Wonderful* Jokes of the Year!

Knock Knock
Who's there?
Wayne
Wayne who?
Wayne in a manger!

Knock Knock
Who's there?
Mary
Mary who?
Mary Christmas!

Knock Knock
Who's there?
Olive
Olive who?
Olive the other reindeer, used to laugh and call him names!

*It's Christmas - the jokes are supposed to be bad!!!

Name the Christmas Film #1

> **CHRISTMAS**

▶ **CHRISTMAS**

Find the answer at the bottom of the next page.

The Search is on for Christmas

Can you find the Christmassy words?

```
K I E L X E U M R U E I I T Z S
N O I T A R O C E D M P A M L C
Q Q K F D K P T J T I L C A G R
Y G S D X Y R E E H M Y V P U O
R V F C V F C S R L O I L Z K O
R G X A P N I B O Y T J R L U G
E N A T I V I T Y S N S K W O E
M C A M S H P U E Q A U I I H H
J B M A Q H B F L W P K G M Q F
Z Y G G J Q O C M O L O N K I A
A K Z K B A I P A M T C D Q W P
X T K M A H F Z P I E J V E Z X
H A U O A S D N N I S K E J V L
N D T L G A E S I O N K C R O E
L O R A C T E K W T X G A G C P
V I W S R L S A N T A K W F Z L
```

CAROL, DECORATION, EVE, FESTIVAL, HOLLY, MERRY, MINCE, MISTLETOE, NATIVITY, PANTOMIME, SANTA, SCROOGE, SHOPPING, TINSEL

Look up, down, sideways, diagonally and backwards
Solution on page 114.

Name The Film #1: White Christmas

Your 1940s Must-Have Toy!

Slinky

Who wouldn't want a big metal coil for Christmas? In the 1940s the big toy was a steel spring that could "walk"!

The Slinky was invented by accident, when engineer Richard James knocked a spring off his desk. He watched as it 'stepped' off a stack of books, then off the table, onto the floor, before coiling back into position.

James realized that the kids might be impressed with this (remember they didn't have PlayStations in the olden days), so he set about creating the perfect toy spring. A few hundred million sales later, and it's clear to see why the Slinky is our must-have toy for the 1940s.

12 Days of Christmas for budding Scrooges!

Every year some fancy firm that has something to do with money, tells us how much it costs to buy all the gifts from the Twelve Days of Christmas. Apparently they reckon it's now over £60,000! We love a challenge, so we decided to try and find the 12 days of gifts for the smallest price possible. If any of you are in love, but you've not got much cash, here's our alternative list:

A Partridge in a Pear Tree

An easy one to start - we headed onto Amazon and bought Alan Partridge: Alpha Papa on DVD for 9·1p (plus £1.26 postage).

We then got a packet of Pear Tree seeds from the local garden centre for £2 (love is all about patience) and we were on our way! **Total so far: £4.20**

Two Turtle Doves

We tried gluing wings on our pet turtles*, but that didn't work, so we found a lovely little ornament on eBay for £19.99. **Total so far: £24.19**

*no we didn't. In fact we can safely say that no animals were harmed during the writing of this book.

Three French Hens

We found a great ale brewed by The Bruery, called Trois Poules Français. (That's Three French Hens for those of you who aren't as cultured as what we are). Apparently it's a 'satisfyingly tart, dark ale with hints of oak and dried fruit that finishes with a clean, vinous character typical of a deep red wine'. Annoyingly, it was a limited edition, now sold out, but we spotted a bottle on an auction site for £30! **Total so far: £54.19**

Four Calling Birds

Now this is where we might have got a little bit creative. Ever watch gangster movies? Heard the phrase used when one gangster tells tales about the other gangsters, 'sing like a canary'? Well, obviously we weren't going to speak to any real gangsters, but we did head down to our local pub. We persuaded four of the regulars to tell tales about each other for £10 each. So that's 4 x £10 = £40. **Total so far £94.19**

Five Gold Rings

These are supposed to cost hundreds of pounds each, but we found some at Argos for £8 each. They're genuine Stainless Steel Gold, which sounds good to us, so that's 5 x £8, and another £40 spent. **Total so far: £134.19**

Six Geese a-Laying

No-one actually wants to get a real live goose for Christmas, never mind six of them! But the mention of "a-laying" got us thinking. What better way to prove that six geese are a-laying, than provide the evidence - six goose eggs. We had to find a fancy farm store, but for £12 + £5 postage, we had six goose eggs (and the next day we had a really, really, really big omelette). **Total so far: £151.19**

Seven Swans a-Swimming

This is where we really start saving you money. Get yourself down to your local park pond* and feast your eyes on some swans for free. Cost: £0. **Total so far: £151.19**

*swans not available at all parks. Please check park website for details.

Eight Maids a-Milking

We had to go to eight different coffee shops and drink eight different Lattes, but we did see eight 'maids' 'a-milking' our milky coffees. This one is a bit awkward as you have to hang around till you're sure you'll be served by a woman (or the Latte count will add up), and when you are being served, you really have to make sure you don't call your barista 'maid'. £2.85 x 8 = £22.80. **Total so far: £173.99**

Nine Ladies Dancing

Nine? How about ninety!? We just headed off to a local nightclub, grabbed a seat with a view of the dancefloor, and started counting. £10 entry. £4 for the drink. A few difficult conversations with jealous boyfriends were free. So our **total so far is £187.99**

Ten Lords a-Leaping

Unless you live near the House of Lords in London, it's actually quite tricky to find ten Lords in one place at the same time. So we made our own.

There are plenty of sites selling land in Scotland, but it looked a bit dodgy to us, so we headed off to the Sealand website. Before you phone PETA, this isn't a place where large Whales perform tricks, but a genuine(ish) micro-nation off the coast of England. It's actually a bit of metal in the sea, but they've had a battle, charges of treason, a government in exile, AND they sell Lordships for £29.99. We found ten friends who were physically fit enough to leap, and turned them into Lords in return for a co-ordinated jump about. This was our most expensive item at £299.90, so the **total so far jumps up to £487.89**

Eleven Pipers Piping

Having blown our budget on the Lords we were looking to save money here. Head to YouTube, Search for "The Massed Pipes and Drums - Edinburgh Military Tattoo - BBC One" and you'll see pipers, pipers, and more pipers (and drummers) - all for free! **Total so far: £487.89**

Twelve Drummers Drumming

Now we could have just counted the drummers in that last YouTube clip, but, even by our low standards, that didn't feel right. Fortunately if you live in a city you're never far from a swarm of hipsters these days, and where there are beards, there will be Djembe drummers. We got lucky and found a drumming group on meetup.com. There was a charge of £10 to hire the drums (apparently they thought it was 'odd' that we just wanted to watch, so we had to join in), but as that's the last item on our list, we were happy to pay!

Final total: £497.89

As you can see, we've already saved you £59,502.11, so if you want someone to look after your money, ask us*, and not some fancy firm.

*Please don't ask us, we are very irresponsible.

You call him Santa...

...but that's not the whole story. A monk called Saint Nicholas (born in the 3rd Century) is considered the source of many Santa Claus legends. He was a Greek Christian Bishop and came from an area that is now part of Turkey. He was well known for giving secret gifts (although how you become well known for doing secret things is a mystery to us!). His gift giving included leaving coins in shoes that people left out - something that is still a tradition in some countries today. The story goes that if you mumble his name really fast it sounds a bit like Santa Claus - which is proof in our book.

So, was he really Santa? If you want to know the truth, why not wait up on Christmas Eve and ask him yourself?

Deck the Halls with Lots of Jokes... L-o-l-o-l O-l-o-l

What do Mexican Snowmen eat?

Brrrrrr-itos!

What do you get when you eat all the Christmas decorations?

Tinsel-itus

How does Santa relax in the evenings?

He has a bauble bath.

A Random Top 10 – UK Box Office Christmas 2005

1. The Chronicles of Narnia: The Lion, the Witch and the Wardrobe

2. King Kong

3. Harry Potter and the Goblet of Fire

4. Lassie

5. Dosti

6. The Family Stone

7. Flightplan

8. March of the Penguins

9. Polar Express

10. Bluff Master

Christmas on the Telly Quiz

1. Christmas Comes But Once a Year sees Don Draper of Mad Men 'celebrate' Christmas. Which actor plays Don? Jon Boeuf, Jon Lamb, or Jon Hamm?

2. Steve Coogan played Alan Partridge in a Knowing Me, Knowing You special for Christmas 1995. It was called a Partridge in a Pear Tree. True or False?

3. Del Boy and Rodney famously chased off a gang of muggers while dressed as Batman and Robin in a Christmas episode of Only Fools and Horses. What was the episode called? Bat-Del and Rod-Boy, Heroes and Villains or The Fancy Dress Party?

4. A Charlie Brown Christmas was a TV highlight for kids in 1965, and for many millions since. For a Christmas Quiz Point, who created Charlie Brown? Jerry B. Katz, Charles M. Schulz, or Charles G. Brown?

5. And for a bonus, what was Charlie Brown's dog called?

6. A headless snowman is caught by Mystery Inc. in whose Christmas special?

7. And for a bonus, can you name all the members of Mystery Inc.?

8. In Blackadder's Christmas Carol, who plans to give Ebenezer Blackadder a £50,000 reward for being 'the nicest man in England'?

Answers on page 100

A Very, Very Old Card

The very first Christmas cards were sold in 1843 in London. They had a picture of a family drinking wine, drawn by John Callcott Horsley. The cards were commissioned by Sir Henry Cole and sold for a shilling (Ye Olde Englishe Monie) each.

That was actually quite a lot of money at the time (about a week's wages), but if you want to buy one now you'll have to pay a LOT more. There are only about a dozen of the original cards left and one was sold in 2001 for £20,000. So, if someone sends you one this Christmas, you might want to look after it!

Name the Christmas Tune #2

Find the answer at the bottom of page 38.

Your 1950s Must-Have Toy!

The Hula Hoop

If the phrase 'You know, for kids' means nothing to you, then you must go and watch the movie The Hudsucker Proxy right now. We can wait. La, la, la. Tum-de-tum. Ok, have you watched it? Good, so you'll know that Norville Barnes invented the Hula Hoop and made Hudsucker Industries a ton of money. You'll also know that he invented the Frisbee.

Sadly, that's not quite true, it's just a movie. But the modern day Hula Hoop - the one we know and love - was invented in the 1950s. In fact it was created by Richard Knerr and Arthur "Spud" Melin and sold by the Wham-O toy company. It wasn't a new idea, as children (and adults) had been 'hooping' since time began (or for at least 600 years, whichever is earlier), but that didn't stop them selling millions!

If Santa was a Jigsaw

An Elf has made a terrible mistake. He's put some extra jigsaw pieces in your puzzle and now you don't know which one to use.

Which jigsaw piece completes Santa's face?

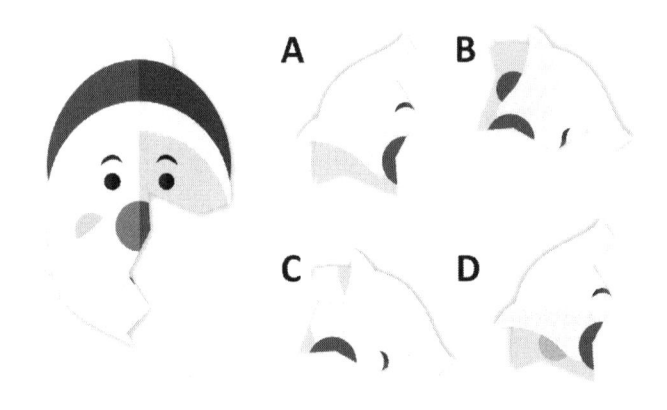

See page 118 for the answer.

Name The Tune #2: Santa Baby

Beware Krampus!

In the midst of Europe, you'd better not be naughty, as Santa has a little help. Say hello to Krampus! In many European countries (especially those in the Alps), this horned gentleman (or goat-like beast, if you prefer), has some kind of sub-contracting arrangement with Santa, and deals with the naughty list himself. That worries us! As a specialist in dealing with naughty children his cruel presents are bound to be scarier than the busy Santa, who clearly prefers to concentrate on the good kids.

And if the real thing doesn't sound bad enough, in some countries adults will dress up as Krampus, drink too much (and we're not talking water or milk!), and chase everyone else through the streets in a celebration called Krampuslauf!

Feed the Elves
and they will come!

Now we all know that we're supposed to leave snacks out for Santa and his reindeer - but what about the poor elves? Surely there must be a few elves in the sleigh alongside the old man? Elves are small. We know that. So what do you feed elves? Of course, Small Elf Food!

Elf Doughnuts - melt a little chocolate and drizzle it over cheerios to make mini elf doughnuts! (If you're not a grown-up, or you are a grown-up, but can't be trusted with hot things, then ask someone responsible to do this).

Elf Drinks - Use the lid of an old toothpaste tube (or similar - those ones that aren't flip-top lids). Clean it well, and use it as a mini cup.

Christmas Day People: The Quiz

1. Annie Lennox, born on Christmas Day 1954, had a huge hit with Sweet Dreams (Are Made of This), but what was the name of her band? The Stylistics, The Realistics, or The Eurythmics?

2. Carrie was the first novel by Steven King, and when it was made into a film, no-one would have imagined that it would be the first of more than 100 different film/tv adaptations of his work. But what's this got to do with Christmas? Well, the star of Carrie was born on 25th December 1949 - can you name her?

3. The famous Spanish painter Joan Miró died on 25th December 1983, having lived to the fine old age of 90. What style did he use for his most famous paintings: Impressionism, Surrealism or Realism?

4. Fairytale of New York is one of the biggest Christmas hits of all time in the UK, despite its less than cheerful lyrics. But which of its two singers was born on the 25th December? Shane MacGowan or Kirsty MacColl?

5. Charlie Chaplin died on Christmas day in 1977. What was the name of his most famous character? The Little Drifter, The Man in the Hat, or The Little Tramp?

6. Considered by many to be the greatest physicist that ever lived, Isaac Newton was born on Christmas Day 1642. One of his greatest achievements was the theory of gravitation – but according to legend, what inspired this theory?

7. And for an Isaac Newton bonus: If you want to give a present to a big Newton fan then you might want to track down a ring, created in the 19th century using part of his body. Which part was used?

8. Humphrey Bogart was another Christmas baby – born in 1899. He's made some wonderful movies, but can you name the 'bird' he was chasing in a 1941 film directed by John Huston?

9. Which famous American comedian, who died on Christmas Day 1946, once said, "If at first you don't succeed, try, try again. Then quit. There's no point in being a fool about it."? Groucho Marks, W. C. Fields, or Jerry Seinfeld?

10. Which founder of a famous car manufacturer was born on Christmas Day? Henry Ford, Horace Elgin Dodge or Louis Chevrolet?

Answers on page 102

Name the Christmas Tune #3

```
SITUATION REPORT...

Weather
STATUS: FRIGHTFUL

Heating Situation
STATUS: DELIGHTFUL

Alternate Locations
STATUS: NONE
```

Find the answer at the bottom of page 46.

Rudolph the Bacterial Nosed Reindeer

Why does Rudolph have a red nose? Well, scientists have thought long and hard about this, and have come up with two answers - which do you think is true?

The Red Blood Cell Hypothesis - Reindeer have 25% more blood vessels in their noses, so when they exercise blood is pumped around their body quickly, and their noses turn red.

The Bacterial Hypothesis - Rudolph is no ordinary reindeer, but has a special bioluminescent bacteria growing in his nose. This bacteria glows in the dark! Now this may sound more unlikely, but the phenomenon does exist in nature, and can be seen on the Hawaiian Bobtail Squid, which uses its glow in the dark abilities to hunt at night.

Which is true about Rudolph? Only Santa knows for sure!

Quick!
Hide the Broom!

One of our favourite Christmas tales is a story of hidden Norwegian Brooms.

We read of a superstition in Norway, which talks of witches and other creatures of the night. They search the towns and villages on Christmas Eve, looking for brooms to steal. Their plan is to use the brooms to ride around on, and get up to no good. One version of the tale suggests the witches planned to ride around from house to house stealing presents from children! The Norwegians couldn't let this happen, so on Christmas Eve they made sure all their brooms were safely hidden.

Your 1960s Must-Have Toy!

Barrel of Monkeys

A barrel.

Inside are monkeys.

Not real monkeys, but monkeys made out of plastic.

Sometimes the greatest inventions sound a bit silly when you try to explain them on paper.

So we won't try.

All we'll say is, if you were a kid in the 60s and you didn't have a barrel filled with monkeys, then you missed out.

And if you want to know more, then according to Wikipedia, there is a North American Barrel of Monkeys Association.

But we don't believe them.

Hcrismtsa lla imdex pu

We've mixed up the letter of some very Christmassy films - Can you work out what they are? And while you're at it, can you work out the name of this quiz?

1. jilgen lla teh wya

2. het antas sacule

3. fle

4. teh minrgthae eofber mrihctssa

5. liadoyh nin

6. sthcirsam whit eth rkkans

7. sti a ryev emryr etupmp hcaritsms

8. ourf sisrcteamssh

9. hte maylif noste

10. ocseogdr

You can find the answers on page 119.

48

Hello? Hello? Is that Santa? Can I speak to an elf please?

If you want to know where Santa is on Christmas Eve then you can head on over to the NORAD website (that's the North American Aerospace Defense Command!) and track his progress across the globe. Now, how many of you know why NORAD are only doing this because of a misdirected telephone call?

In the 1950s, Sears department store in Colorado Springs would run a Christmas advert each year asking children to call Santa on his private phone. However, in 1955, a misprint in the ad meant that instead of reaching Santa, children were calling US Air Force Colonel Harry Shoup of NORAD* on a top secret 'crisis' hotline!

"Is this Santa Claus?" the little voice asked.

That little voice was the first of MANY, and soon the phone was ringing constantly. Initially Colonel Shoup was annoyed – this was an important phone line – but the calls weren't going to stop, so he told one of the Airmen under his command to answer the calls, and "pretend you're Santa".

Before long, they were giving the kids information on where Santa's sleigh was - after all, their job was to track unusual aerospace movements - and a tradition was born.

·It was actually called CONAD at the time, but we never let an acronym get in the way of our story telling!

How does Santa deliver all those presents in one night?

A research study calculated how fast Santa would have to travel to deliver all his presents in one night. The finest brains used the finest computers and the sharpest pencils to work out that Santa would have to visit 822 homes each second! That means he'd be travelling at two million, three hundred and forty thousand miles an hour.

Just as well Santa is magic, isn't it?

A Random Top 10 - Merry Christmas and a Happy New Year* in 10 languages!

1. Buon Natale e Felice Anno Nuovo (Italian)

2. Crăciun Fericit și La multi ani (Romanian)

3. Feliz Natal e um Feliz Ano Novo (Portuguese)

4. Gëzuar Krishtlindjet dhe Vitin e Ri (Albanian)

5. Glædelig jul og godt nytår! or simply God jul (Danish)

6. God Jul och Gott Nytt År (Swedish)

7. Joyeux Noël et Bonne Année (French)

8. Nadolig Llawen a Blwyddyn Newydd Dda (Welsh)

9. Nollaig Shona Duit (Irish)

10. Selamat Hari Natal dan Tahun Baru (Indonesian)

*probably.

Name the Christmas Tune #4

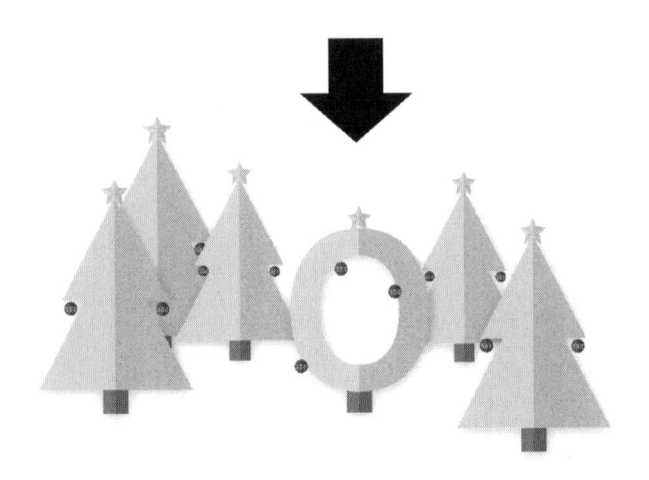

Find the answer at the bottom of page 54.

Jokin' Around the Christmas Tree

Why don't Snowmen drive cars?

They prefer to ride an 'icicle.

Who is the meanest reindeer?

Rude-olph!

Why did Santa throw out his pants?

Because he found a ho-ho-hole in them!

What do call a cat on the beach?

Sandy Claws

Your 1970s Must-Have Toy!

Weebles Wobble, but they don't fall down.

Apparently there is a LOT of science that went into making our 'must-have toy' of the 1970s. Weebles were little plastic people that had no legs. Instead they were round - but not just any kind of round. They were "special science round". The kind of round that means they wobble... but they don't fall down.

Now that's Christmas magic - so they win our 1970s must-have toy prize!

Name That Tune #1: O Christmas Tree

The 'Once upon a time some authors wrote about Christmas' Quiz

1. A Christmas Carol is one of our favourite seasonal books. The story tells of a mean old man visited by four ghosts. Can you name the ghosts?

2. The Sugar Plum Fairy dances in which Christmas ballet? Swan Lake, The Nutcracker or The Sleeping Beauty?

3. Who wrote the seasonal tale of the Little Match Girl? The Brothers Grimm, J. K. Rowling or Hans Christian Andersen?

4. L. Frank Baum wrote a tale of A Kidnapped Santa Claus - but he's MUCH more famous for another book, which became one of the greatest children's films of all time. What was the book?

5. We've all heard of Rudolph the red-nosed reindeer, but in the poem A Visit from St Nicholas, more often known by its first line 'Twas the night before Christmas, Santa had eight other reindeer. Can you name them?

6. The Adventure of the Blue Carbuncle was a Christmas themed Sherlock Holmes Mystery. Can you name Sherlock's medically trained partner?

7. For a Sherlock Holmes bonus, who wrote the original books? Arthur C. Clarke, Arthur Conan Doyle, or Robert Louis Stevenson?

8. Which of these three Christmas movies isn't based on a book? The Polar Express, Elf, or How the Grinch Stole Christmas?

See page 106 for the answers.

O Star of wonder,
Star of night,
Are you a comet or
a form of planetary light?

Astronomers have come up with many theories about the Star of Bethlehem over the years. We've been told the star could have been a planetary conjunction involving various combinations of Jupiter, Venus and Saturn along with stars from other galaxies, a comet, a supernova, a heliacal rising, a double occultation, and even Rudolph's nose* – but which do you think is the truth?

*OK, we made that one up.

The Penny Magician

For this trick you'll need ten pennies, all with different issue years. You'll also need a Santa Hat to put them in (if you don't have a Santa hat, a Christmas stocking, other hat, or any small bag/purse will do).

Place the pennies on a table and ask someone to check that they are all different years.

Then ask them to place the pennies in the hat and tell them to select someone else to choose a coin from the hat, while you turn away.

Tell them that you're going to ask Santa to help you find the penny with a little Christmas magic.

Ask each person in turn to take the coin, note the date on it, and then hold it tightly in their hand while saying the magic words:

"SANTA, SANTA, SANTA, MAKE THIS THE CHRISTMAS PENNY".

When the last person has done this ask them to put the penny back into the hat and return in to you.

Place your hand in the bag, close your eyes, and say the magic words:

"SANTA, SANTA, SANTA, SHOW ME THE CHRISTMAS PENNY".

How will you find the penny? Simple - It's been passed around and held tightly in a few warm hands, so will be much warmer than the other pennies.

Show the audience the penny and take a bow!

12 Days of Wordsearch

Your true love has sent you a puzzle.
How fast can you solve it?

```
O X B Y R J D H O S Q P M S R R
S O E A Y J U H O A M M N D Q I
T W E L V E S N A W S K S R F N
V P E J G N S G R Q U C A O B G
E A F B U R D R Z D D W N L N S
N Y V I I G Y P S S U A U J S I
D L O H E N S O R D F B Y G E A
S L V E Z W W E S A I F X S I Z
J R S T S J P C B J Y A B P D Z
P E E L I I B G U E M A M G A A
O F H M P E R I I A G X M E L E
F L W R M K K U R Q I G Q G N A
P T W N M U A S M D Q Z Z M K N
E G D I R T R A P W S P X N L C
T G V I E X I D X P J Y G D K H
F M W L B D M I T R K B E N M Z
```

BIRDS, DAYS, DRUMMERS, GEESE, HENS, LADIES, LORDS, MAIDS, PARTRIDGE, PEAR, PIPERS, RINGS, SWANS, TWELVE

Look up, down, sideways, diagonally and backwards
Solution on page 115.

Name the Christmas Film #2

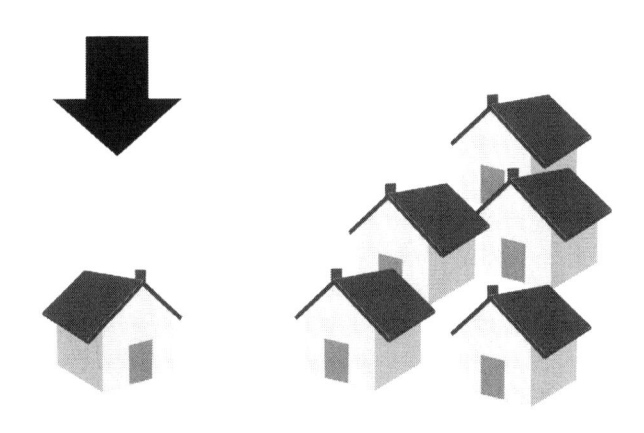

Find the answer at the bottom of the next page.

Japan ♥ KFC @ Christmas

Christmas is one holiday that isn't big in Japan. Only a small percentage of the population are Christians and 25th December isn't even a national holiday. However that doesn't mean they don't have any unusual Christmas traditions. KFC is huge in Japan, and in 1974 they ran an advertising campaign built around the slogan "Christmas = Kentucky!" or "Kurisumasu ni wa kentakkii!" if you speak Japanese*. The idea took hold, and now the biggest Fried Chicken day of the year is Christmas Day!

*We don't, so it may well say "Let's see if we can convince the silly foreigners that we eat KFC at Christmas!", which in some ways we hope it does.

In other Fried Chicken related Christmas news (yes, there is some!), did you know that Colonel Sanders has released a number of Christmas albums? Our research suggests he didn't sing on them himself, but we truly hope they play them in Japanese branches of KFC all year round.

We Wish You a Joking Christmas!

Who says Oh Oh Oh?

Santa walking backwards!

What's the difference between Santa's reindeer and a Knight?

One slays the dragon, and the other's draggin' the sleigh

Where does a snowman keep his money?

In a snow bank.

Where do Snowmen like to dance?

At Snowballs.

He was (possibly not) born on Christmas Day!

We all know that Christmas is a celebration of Jesus' birthday - but a lot of religious scholars now believe Jesus was born at another time of year, with September being one popular choice.

So, why Christmas day? Well, there is some evidence from the 2nd century AD, that 25th December was considered the date of Jesus' birth by some Christians. It's also close to Epiphany (6th January) - an important day for many Christians which celebrates the visit of the three wise men/kings. There was also a pagan festival around the same time in late December, and it's likely all these factors resulted in the Church settling on the 25th.

After all these years it's just as much a Christian festival as it ever was a pagan one, and in many places around the world it's becoming an important date even to non-Christians.

So, wherever you are, and whatever you believe, we hope you're having a good Christmas!

Your 1980s Must-Have Toy!

Cabbage Patch Kids

Not just a soft toy. If you "bought" one of these dolls, or were lucky enough that Santa gave you one, then you were officially the doll's parent. There were adoption papers and everything.

Originally called Little People, they were created by an artist called Xavier Roberts (who was apparently inspired by another doll maker Martha Nelson Thomas). The dolls were so popular that there were fights at stores between parents trying to buy dolls for their kids (I assume these were already naughty parents who knew that Santa Claus wouldn't be bringing them a doll any time soon). These store fights became known as The Cabbage Patch Riots! Any toy that can cause a riot must be worthy of a place in our 'must-have' list!

Big Box, Little Box, Cardboard Fish?

Ah Christmas... a time for giving. They say 'it's better to give than receive', and we agree... especially if your gift is a prank. You get to give the gift, and receive a laugh!

Big Box Little Gift - First, find the smallest gift possible. It can be something brilliant, or if you're short of cash, it can be a chocolate bar! Now find the biggest box possible. Place small gift in big box. Fill space in box with old newspaper. Wrap to a high standard. Wait till Christmas day.

The Forrest Gump - An Empty Box of Chocolates - If you're feeling particularly naughty (and don't mind being on Santa's list for the following year), then how about buying a nice box of chocolates. Eat them all, then put cut up pieces of carrot in their place. Don't do this too far before Christmas unless you want a really rotten present.

Eat, Drink & Be Merry: The Quiz

1. What Christmas drink often involves spirits, such as rum or brandy being added to a milky drink?

2. What is the name of the traditional Italian Christmas bread loaf?

3. What do Norwegians call the warmed wine they drink at Christmas time? Gløgg, Gøøgle, or Grølsch?

4. Puto Bumbong is a purple sticky rice cake, eaten at Christmas in which country? The Philippines, Ghana, or Peru?

5. Szaloncukor is popular in Hungary at Christmas - but what is it? A sausage, a drink, or a sweet?

6. In Britain, pig's head smothered in mustard used to be a popular Christmas dish. True or False?

7. What is Stollen? A Finnish name for Santa, a German fruit cake, or a word we've just made up?

8. Poor turkeys don't do well out of Christmas, but it used to be worse for them. In the 18th Century, not only were tens of thousands eaten each year in London, but they had to walk there from the turkey farms in Norfolk - a distance of up to 100 miles. What did they wear to help them during the journey?

See page 109 for the answers.

Large Swedish Goats

Gävle, in Sweden, is home to the biggest Christmas Goat in the World: Gävle Goat. Yes, you read that right. The biggest Christmas Goat in the world. It's 13 meters high and every few years someone sets fire to him. The Swedes don't seem to mind and the goat enjoys the fame - he's even got twitter and an email address.

•Now, before we started our research for this book we were unaware that there was such a thing as Christmas goats. However, we have now realized that we actually own a Christmas goat, which we bought from Ikea. We thought it was a reindeer, or a horse, but now we know it's a goat. It is not the biggest in the world though, so don't plan a visit to our house.

Cleverer than a
Santa with two brains?

Here's a puzzle so hard that some of you might still be working it out NEXT Christmas!

Five of Santa's best elves missed the Elf Train, and now must make their own way to the North Pole. Each elf will arrive on a different day in December, will travel in a different way, and will make a different toy for the boys and girls. Follow the clues on the next page, then work out:

Which Elf will arrive on December 22nd?

Who will travel by reindeer?

Who will make the Teddy Bear?

CLUES

1. Sugarplum won't take the Sleigh.

2. Chipper will arrive two days after Buddy.

3. The elf that makes train sets won't arrive by snowmobile.

4. The elf on snowmobile will arrive before the elf on the sleigh.

5. The elf that makes Yoyos will be at the North Pole three days before the elf on the snowmobile.

6. Chipper doesn't make train sets.

7. Of the elf who will arrive on December 23rd and the elf that makes jigsaws, one will arrive on a dog sled and the other is Tootsie.

8. Chipper will use skis to get to the North Pole.

9. Tootsie doesn't make Teddy Bears.

If you've got a brain as big as Santa's belly then you can solve the puzzle in your head. If you're like us you might want to use the grid on the next page.

PUZZLE GRID: Put a tick in a box you know is true, and a cross in a box that can't be. So for clue 1, you'd put a cross where Sugarplum meets Sleigh, as Sugarplum won't take the Sleigh. For clue 2, if Chipper will arrive two days after Buddy, you straight away know Chipper can't arrive on the first two days, so put crosses where Chipper meets the 20th and 21st. Remember, when you know something for sure, that also rules out other options. Use a pencil and have a rubber handy!

	20th	21st	22nd	23rd	24th	Train Set	Toy Soldier	Yoyo	Teddy Bear	Jigsaw	Sleigh	Reindeer	Skis	Snowmobile	Dog Sled
Chipper															
Sugarplum															
Tootsie															
Buddy															
Pixie															
Sleigh															
Reindeer															
Skis															
Snowmobile															
Dog Sled															
Train Set															
Toy Soldier															
Yoyo															
Teddy Bear															
Jigsaw															

See page 120 for the answers.

Name the Christmas Tune #5

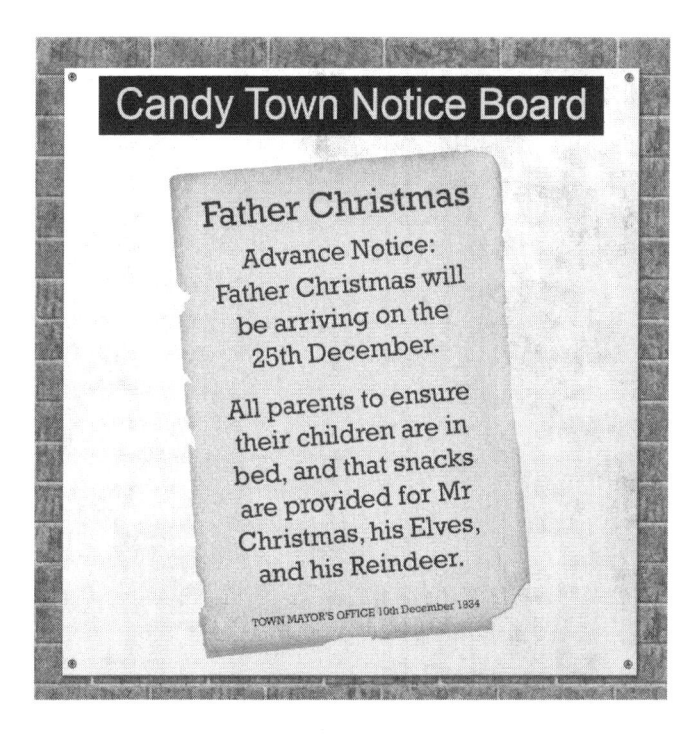

Candy Town Notice Board

Father Christmas

Advance Notice:
Father Christmas will be arriving on the 25th December.

All parents to ensure their children are in bed, and that snacks are provided for Mr Christmas, his Elves, and his Reindeer.

TOWN MAYOR'S OFFICE 10th December 1934

Find the answer at the bottom of the next page.

You Saw Mommy Kissing Who?!

The song "I Saw Mommy Kissing Santa Claus" caused controversy despite it being simply about a husband and wife kissing. Church leaders in Boston condemned the song as immoral, with the rumour being that they thought it was the real Santa doing the kissing! The executive of the record company that released the song, Mitch Miller, worried that the song might get banned all over America, (the cynical might suggest he spotted an opportunity for a little free publicity) and so decided to take action. The song's singer Jimmy Boyd was sent to meet the head of the Catholic Church in Boston (with TV cameras following) to explain the real story behind the song; that "Santa" was in fact the boy's father dressed up, and that he was allowed to kiss his own wife.

Joking in the Air!

Why did the turkey cross the road?

He was playing chicken.

How can you tell if Santa's been hiding in your fridge?

There are boot prints in the butter.

What do they sing at a snowman's birthday party?

Freeze a jolly good fellow.

What do you call an old snowman?

Water.

Who Gets Their Presents First?

The kids of Kiritimati could be considered the luckiest on Earth - for they get to celebrate Christmas Day first. Kiritimati, part of the Republic of Kiribati, is a small• coral atoll in the Pacific Ocean, and it's the first place that the clock ticks past midnight on December 24th. If you check it out on a map, you'll notice something a little odd - the International Date Line is a long way from Kiritimati - around 1500 miles away. In fact, it should be one of the last places on Earth to start each day, but they've bent the date line so that their kids get their presents first.

•It's actually really big for a coral atoll so we're told.

A Random Top 10 – UK Charts Christmas 1980

1. St Winifred's School Choir - There's No One Quite Like Grandma
2. John Lennon* - (Just Like) Starting Over
3. Jona Lewie - Stop The Cavalry
4. John* And Yoko And The Plastic Ono Band With The Harlem Community Choir - Happy Xmas (War Is Over)
5. Abba - Super Trouper
6. Police - De Do Do Do De Da Da Da
7. Adam And The Ants - Antmusic
8. Madness - Embarrassment
9. John Lennon* - Imagine
10. Stray Cats - Runaway Boys

*Sadly John Lennon died in December 1980, which is why he had so many songs in the Christmas top 10 that year.

Some Tree-mendous Facts

Tasty Trees - Ever been tempted to eat your Christmas tree? Thought not. But apparently you can, and they're even rich in vitamins. We wouldn't suggest it unless you're desperate as they may well be covered in an extra layer of not so yummy chemicals to keep away pests (the tiny insect variety, not the child variety).

Mmm... bugs - And that's not the only reason you might want to put that Christmas Tree based snack on hold. Scientists say that up to TWENTY-FIVE THOUSAND insects could be living in the tree - for those insect lovers out there, that's a huge feast of lice, moths and mites. What's more they were probably sleeping in the cold, but once inside your nice warm home... they wake up! The good news is that they're mostly too tiny for us to notice, and they don't eat presents or baubles!

Takk* - Every year since 1947 the city of Oslo in Norway has sent a Christmas Tree to Britain. The trees are a gift, thanking the British for their help during World War II, and are displayed in Trafalgar Square. *That's Norwegian for 'thanks'.

An Even More Random Top 10 – Some Trees

1. Douglas Fir
2. Norway Spruce
3. Leyland Cyprus
4. Artificial
5. Fraser Fir
6. Scotch Pine
7. Blue Spruce
8. Balsam Fir
9. White Pine
10. Nordmann Fir

Sing-a-long-a-Christmas-quiz

1. What's the worldwide biggest selling Christmas song of all time? White Christmas, All I Want for Christmas Is You, or Last Christmas?

2. Which decidedly odd pairing dueted on a version of Little Drummer Boy in 1977?

3. What colourful Christmas song was made famous by Elvis Presley?

4. Which ex-Beatle sang Happy Xmas (War Is Over)? And for a bonus point, what was the name of the 1979 Christmas song by another ex-Beatle?

5. Nat King Cole sings the line "Chestnuts roasting on an open fire" in which Christmas song?

6. She & Him released an entire album of Christmas tunes in 2011 called "A Very She & Him Christmas". One half of the band is known for her comedy show New Girl - who is 'She'?

7. Jimmy Boyd was the boy who saw "...Mommy Kissing Santa Claus" in the 1950s, but how old was the 'boy' when he recorded the song? 8, 13, or 25?

8. Which singer, who died on Christmas Day 2006, famously sang "Get Up"?

9. Christmas songs are usually associated with pop acts, but which alternative rock band released a yearly Christmas song? Coldplay, Radiohead or The Killers?

10. Which family group released a version of 'Santa Claus is Coming to Town' in 1970? The Jackson 5 or The Osmonds?

11. For a bonus point, the musical notes on the previous page are from a well known Christmas song. Do you know which one?

Find the answers on page 111.

Jingle Bells, Jingle Bells, Joking All the Way!

What do you call a blind reindeer?

No eye deer

What do you call a blind reindeer when it's sleeping?

Still no eye deer

If you cross a vampire and a snowman, what do you get?

Frostbite.

What do call Santa when he's having a break?

Santa Pause!

It's a Wonderful Wordsearch!

Find all the Christmassy words hidden in the grid below.

```
M C N C Y T Z K F L Y O D X G V
U R X F U V F N P R E B V T B S
A P F R J Y T J E D G F T I U Q
O W K L F D X E Q I I D R A C C
H E U N D E D R Z C F N Y E B R
Y T O M U N A X X K T O M H T P
Z T A A I Y P S K E U S M N O G
P B C E S A S U T N C B E L L S
Q E R Q R T A X K S A V R N E H
P V D W U W O Z T B D N G C B M
L H E G B Y E C D A W A X X S F
J Q R B X W L N K G J H W Q U H
N S P B E D B Q G I Y U D G X O
H G I E L S U P U M N R L X G J
B I R T H D A Y N F B G S R Q B
D I Y O P C B L W M R R V A Y I
```

ADVENT, BAUBLE, BELLS, BIRTHDAY, CARD, DICKENS, FEAST, GIFT, HYMN, REINDEER, SLEIGH, STOCKING, TURKEY, WREATH

Look up, down, sideways, diagonally and backwards
Solution on page 116.

Selling Christmas

The Ninth Reindeer - Father Christmas originally had eight reindeers but since 1939 he's had nine. That ninth reindeer is Rudolph, probably the most famous of them all, and he was created for US retailers Montgomery Ward as part of a Christmas promotion campaign. One of their copywriters, Bob May, wrote the poem 'Rudolph, the Red-Nosed Reindeer' and millions of copies were distributed. Rudolph almost had another name too - May considered calling him Rollo and Reginald before settling on the name we know him by today!

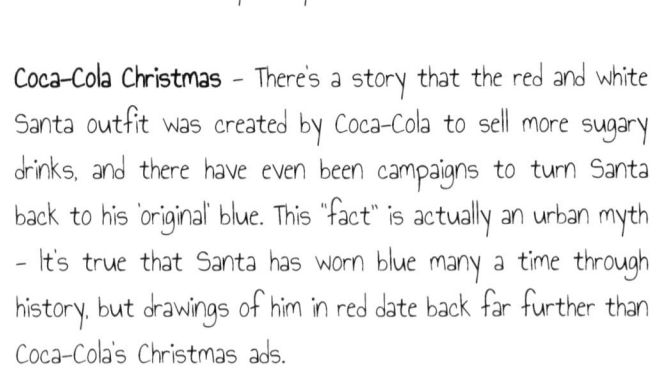

Coca-Cola Christmas - There's a story that the red and white Santa outfit was created by Coca-Cola to sell more sugary drinks, and there have even been campaigns to turn Santa back to his 'original' blue. This "fact" is actually an urban myth - It's true that Santa has worn blue many a time through history, but drawings of him in red date back far further than Coca-Cola's Christmas ads.

Your 1990s Must-Have Toy!

Furby

We were all alive in the 1990s and remember Furby-mania well. But we still can't work out what the furry balls with big eyes actually did. We're told that they spoke some kind of Furby language (Furbish), but, once they were unwrapped on Christmas morning, they began 'learning' the language of their new owners.

Well, we had one and it didn't do much learning at all, so we don't believe a word of this. What's more, we think they looked really weird and we're sure that they gave us nightmares.

So, why is it our 'must-have' toy? Well, if a not very impressive ball of fluff can sell by the tens of millions, we must salute its inventors (and wonder if maybe we were doing something wrong). So, Furby - We salute you!

The Four Elves

Santa is delivering presents to children who live in a tall building. Four of his Elves are helping and these are represented by the four Jacks in a pack of cards.

You'll begin by showing your audience the deck of cards with the four Jacks (Elves) at the back of the deck, fanned out at the top so they can clearly be seen.

Then push the four Jacks back into the pack and place it face down on the table.

Tell your audience the Elves are on top of the building with Santa, but they need to deliver the presents. One by one take the top four cards and place them randomly into the deck.

You can add to your story by saying lines like "Ernie the elf delivers presents to children half way up the building", then place a card half way up. "Alfie the elf delivers to children at the bottom of the building" and place the card nearer the bottom.

Once you've placed all four cards, say "All the presents have been delivered so Santa gives the signal to return to the Sleigh". Knock on the cards, and tell your audience the Elves have returned to the roof.

One by one reveal the top four cards. Each one will be a Jack!

How's it done? At the beginning, when you're preparing the cards with the four Jacks at the back, you actually have four other cards hidden behind them. So long as you don't go too close to your audience, they will assume the Jacks are at the back. When you push the cards back in and place them face down, you'll then be placing these four cards in to the middle of the deck, not the Jacks.

French parents try to ban Father Christmas advert!

What! Banning an ad about Father Christmas? Why, those French!? Oh, wait a minute, turns out they might have had the right idea. An evil* bank in France created an advert which suggested Santa wasn't real! Apart from being a total lie, they also foolishly allowed the ad to be shown during a family film - shattering the Christmas dreams of thousands of French children.

After the parents complained, the bank said that they had no idea it would be shown so early, and although they'd continue showing the ad, it would be later in the evening, when only grown-ups (who KNOW Santa is real) were watching.

*Ok. We admit the bank may not strictly be evil - but we certainly say Boo! Hiss! And Down with this sort of thing!

Fun with Fruit

Dazzle easily impressed people by chopping up fruit in an amusing way.

Christmas Melon Tree - Cut a slice from a watermelon. Then chop the slice into Christmas tree shaped segments. Carefully cut off the skin and then trim the segment of skin so that it can act as a trunk for your melon Christmas tree.

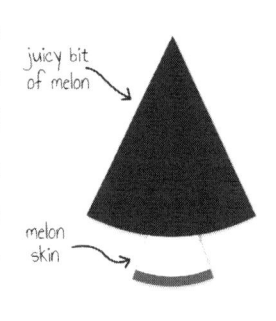

juicy bit of melon

melon skin

Strawberry Father Christmas - Take a strawberry and twist off the stem and leaves. Cut off the bottom third of the strawberry and then place the larger part upside down on your plate. Cover this with a layer of cream and then pop the cut off section back on top, to make Santa's hat. A little extra cream can be added on top for the bobble, and dabs of cream on the front make Santa's coat buttons. Two chocolate drops for eyes and Da daaa!, you've got an anatomically incorrect fruit Santa!

strawberry cut in two

chocolate drop eyes

cream

Name the Christmas Tune #6

➡ **Noël
Noël
Noël
Noël
Noël**

Find the answer at the bottom of page 92.

Happy Birthday to the World Wide Web

While researching this book, we found many, many stories which turned out not to be true. As with Santa's list of nice and naughty children we checked our stories once, then checked them twice, but we still have our suspicions that not every Christmas tale is as it seems.

However, we did want to add one story which we think isn't quite true - and that's the 'fact' that the World Wide Web was 'born' on Christmas Day.

Before we had easy access to so much information, we could have made up half the facts in this book and most people would never know. Now, it's really easy to double-check what's true or not, or is it? We've seen so many stories where there were two versions saying different things, and it's often taken us a while to get to the truth. So, we found it most amusing to discover that one story, that the World Wide Web was 'born on Christmas day', might not be true.

The World Wide Web is a wonderful thing, the source of our new knowledge, but also much confusion, and according to a LOT of different sources, the very first live tests took place on 25th December 1990. However Tim Berners-Lee (known as the father of the World Wide Web), has also said "I was NOT working on Christmas Day" and that the tests were prepared some time before the offices closed for Christmas. The browser did have a version date of 901225 (25th December 1990), but he suggests this was meant to be amusing rather than strictly accurate.

Knowing our luck, we'll discover this interview is rubbish, and that the story was true all along - but in the meantime, we like to think of it as an interesting tale about an interesting Christmas tale.

It's Christmas Day! Here are some Answers!

$$\frac{🎁}{🧝} \times (🍷🍪🍬) + 🧔 = 📅_{25}$$

Answers – Christmas at the Movies Quiz

1. Which Christmas film has made more money at the box office than any other? How the Grinch Stole Christmas, It's a Wonderful Life, or The Polar Express?
   How the Grinch Stole Christmas. Grinch made around £230,000,000 worldwide! It's a Wonderful Life may be a Christmas favourite, but it didn't even cover its budget when it was first released.

2. What were the names of the Cop and the Cab Driver in It's a Wonderful Life? CLUE: This one is easier for Sesame Street fans.
   They were called *Bert and Ernie*. While we'd love to think that this was a subtle tribute to a great film, Jim Henson, creator of the Muppets, claims it was simply a coincidence.

3. What was the name of Macaulay Culkin's character in Home Alone? And for a bonus, what was the name of the 'gang' that he battled with?
   It was *Kevin McCallister* who was left home alone. The gang were called the *'Wet Bandits'* because they left the water running in the houses that they robbed.

4. Scrooged, with Bill Murray, is many people's favourite Christmas movie. But what book was it based on?
It was based on *A Christmas Carol* by Charles Dickens. The book was first published in 1843, and has been the inspiration for many movies over the years.

5. Elf is a modern Christmas Classic. Can you name the four main food groups that Elves eat?
Candy, candy canes, candy corn and syrup. Probably not a diet that your doctor would approve of!

6. The 1930s' classic, Miracle on 34th Street, was remade in 1994. Which dinosaur fan played Santa?
Richard Attenborough. He also played John Hammond, the owner of the original Jurassic Park.

7. Tom Hanks stars as the Conductor in The Polar Express, but who plays Santa Claus in the movie? For a bonus point, who played Scrooge?
Tom Hanks played Santa Claus as well — and for the bonus point, Scrooge was played by *Tom Hanks* too! He kept himself busy that Christmas playing numerous other parts in the movie.

8. Gremlins is slightly darker than your typical Christmas movie — but it's one of our favourites! The star is the cute Mogwai called Gizmo. But what must you never do

to a Mogwai after midnight, no matter how much it cries or begs? Feed it, play with it, or sing to it? *Feed it!* And if you haven't seen the movie we won't tell you what happens - but it's not good!

9. What is the name of the family in National Lampoon's Christmas Vacation? For a bonus who played the family's son, Rusty? CLUE: He's making a big bang as one of the highest paid TV stars of the 2010s!
The Griswolds. Rusty was played by *Johnny Galecki* - best known as Leonard Hofstadter in the Big Bang Theory!

10. Tim Allen stars in The Santa Clause which made a surprising amount of money at the box office. However, he co-stars in another series of movies which were even more successful - yet his face is never seen. Name the movie series and Tim's character.
Toy Story of course! Tim plays *Buzz 'to infinity and beyond' Lightyear*.

Film: Christmas at the Movies
Director: Santa
Date: 25th December
Cameraman: Rudolph

Answers – A Quizzing We Shall Go!

1. What Christmas wonder was invented by Edward Johnson and displayed at his home in New York City in 1882?
   The miniature electric *Christmas tree lights*. He worked for the Edison Electric Light Company and had 80 red, white and blue lights specially made for his tree.

2. In Iceland, children are lucky enough to get visits from more than one gift-giving "Santa" – but how lucky are they? Do they get gifts from 3, 7 or 13 Santas?
   13! In Iceland Santa's duties are undertaken by thirteen different troll-like boys called the Yule Lads. Each lad leaves presents, or something nasty, depending on whether the child has been nice or naughty.

3. During the festive period, it's traditional in many countries to kiss underneath what? Holly, Mistletoe or Eggnog?
   Mistletoe. The tradition (no doubt invented by someone who wasn't getting enough kisses) even suggested it was bad luck to refuse a kiss!

4. If you want to write to Santa in Canada, you use the postal code HOH OHO. True or False?
   True. Letters sent to Santa Claus, North Pole, Canada, HOH OHO will be delivered by the Canadian postal service.

5. In a 1964 movie, Santa had more than a few naughty kids to deal with. Who was Santa's foe? The Venetians, The Moon People, or The Martians?
   The Martians. Santa Claus Conquers the Martians is generally considered one of the worst movies ever made.

6. Which child star said, "I stopped believing in Santa Claus when I was six. Mother took me to see him in a department store and he asked for my autograph". Shirley Temple, Miley Cyrus or Macaulay Culkin?
   Shirley Temple. Shirley is the youngest ever winner of an Oscar - she received an honorary Academy Award at the 1935 ceremony, when she was just six years old!

Answers – Christmas on the Telly Quiz

1. Christmas Comes But Once a Year sees Don Draper of Mad Men 'celebrate' Christmas. Which actor plays Don? Jon Boeuf, Jon Hamm or Jon Lamb?
   John Hamm. The episode title, Christmas Comes But Once a Year, was the name of a song by Stan Freberg, which mocks the way advertising companies use Christmas simply to sell us stuff.

2. Steve Coogan played Alan Partridge in a Knowing Me, Knowing You special for Christmas 1995. It was called a Partridge in a Pear Tree. True or False?
   False. It was called Knowing Me Knowing Yule with Alan Partridge.

3. Del Boy and Rodney famously chased off a gang of muggers while dressed as Batman and Robin in a Christmas episode of Only Fools and Horses. What was the episode called? Bat-Del and Rod-Boy, Heroes and Villains or The Fancy Dress Party?
   Heroes and Villians. In 2001 the episode was voted the top Christmas show of all time.

4. A Charlie Brown Christmas was the TV highlight for kids in 1965, and for many millions since. For a Christmas Quiz Point, who created Charlie Brown? Jerry B. Katz, Charles M. Schulz, or Charles G. Brown?
Charles M. Schulz created the comic strip Peanuts, which starred Charlie Brown.

5. And for a bonus, what was Charlie Brown's dog called?
Charlie's dog is the famous *Snoopy*.

6. A headless snowman is caught by Mystery Inc. in whose Christmas special?
It's Scooby Doo! in the 2002 episode A Scooby-Doo! Christmas.

7. And for a bonus, can you name all the members of Mystery Inc.?
Scooby-Doo, Shaggy Rogers, Fred Jones, Velma Dinkley, and Daphne Blake. If you got the surnames, give yourself an extra candy cane!

8. In Blackadder's Christmas Carol, who plans to give Ebenezer Blackadder a £50,000 reward for being 'the nicest man in England'?
Queen Victoria and Prince Albert – played by Miriam Margoyles and Jim Broadbent. In typical Blackadder fashion, things don't quite work out as planned.

Answers – Christmas Day People: The Quiz

1. Annie Lennox, born on Christmas Day 1954, had a huge hit with Sweet Dreams (Are Made of This), but what was the name her band? The Stylistics, The Realistics, or The Eurythmics?
   The Eurythmics. The duo (Dave Stewart and Annie) had a number 1 hit in the US and reached number 2 in the UK.

2. Carrie was the first novel by Steven King, and when it was made into a film, no-one would have imagined that it would be the first of more than 100 different film/tv adaptations of his work. But what's this got to do with Christmas? Well, the star of Carrie was born on 25th December 1949 – can you name her?
   Sissy Spacek – she was even nominated for an Oscar.

She later won the Best Actress Oscar for her role in Coal Miner's Daughter.

3. The famous Spanish painter Joan Miró died on 25th December 1983, having lived to the fine old age of 90. What style did he use for his most famous paintings: Impressionism, Surrealism or Realism?
Surrealism.

4. Fairytale of New York is one of the biggest Christmas hits of all time in the UK, despite its less than cheerful lyrics. But which of its two singers was born on the 25th December? Shane MacGowan or Kirsty MacColl?
Shane MacGowan – he was born in Kent, in 1957.

5. Charlie Chaplin died on Christmas day in 1977. What was the name of his most famous character? The Little Drifter, The Man in the Hat, or The Little Tramp?
The Little Tramp. Chaplin described the character as "…many-sided, a tramp, a gentleman, a poet, a dreamer, a lonely fellow, always hopeful of romance and adventure. He would have you believe he is a scientist, a musician, a duke, and a polo-player. However, he is not above picking up cigarette-butts or robbing a baby of its candy. And,

of course, if the occasion warrants it, he will kick a lady in the rear — but only in extreme anger!"

6. Considered by many to be the greatest physicist that ever lived, Isaac Newton was born on Christmas Day 1642. One of his greatest achievements was the theory of gravitation - but according to legend, what inspired this theory?
An apple falling from a tree! Newton himself often told this story, so it's likely to have some truth, although not many historians believe that it fell directly on his head.

7. And for an Isaac Newton bonus: If you want to give a present to a big Newton fan then you might want to track down a ring, created in the 19th century using part of his body. Which part was used?
A tooth. And apparently it's the most expensive tooth ever sold — it would be worth approximately £37,000 today.

8. Humphrey Bogart was another Christmas baby - born in 1899. He's made some wonderful movies, but can you name the 'bird' he was chasing in a 1941 film directed by John Huston?
The Maltese Falcon. The Falcon was a "black figure of a

bird", and you'll have to watch the film to know more about its mystery!

9. Which famous American comedian, who died on Christmas Day 1946, once said, "If at first you don't succeed, try, try again. Then quit. There's no point in being a fool about it." Groucho Marks, W. C. Fields, or Jerry Seinfeld?
W. C. Fields – He famously enjoyed the 'spirit' of Christmas, but probably wouldn't have got on with Santa – once saying "Anyone who hates children and animals can't be all bad".

10. Which founder of a famous car manufacturer was born on Christmas Day? Henry Ford, Horace Elgin Dodge or Louis Chevrolet?
Louis Chevrolet. He was born on 25th December 1878 in Switzerland.

Answers –
The 'Once upon a time some authors wrote about Christmas' Quiz

1. A Christmas Carol is one of our favourite seasonal books, in which a mean old man is visited by four ghosts. Can you name them?
   The visitors were *The Ghosts of Christmases Past, Present and Yet to Come*, plus *Jacob Marley* – the mean old man, Ebenezer Scrooge's, ex-business partner.

2. The Sugar Plum Fairy dances in which Christmas ballet? Swan Lake, The Nutcracker or The Sleeping Beauty?
   The Nutcracker by Tchaikovsky.

3. Who wrote the seasonal tale of the Little Match Girl? The Brothers Grimm, J. K. Rowling or Hans Christian Andersen?
   Hans Christian Andersen. The tale is both sad and beautiful, one of Anderson's finest.

4. L. Frank Baum wrote a tale of A Kidnapped Santa Claus – but he's MUCH more famous for another book, which became one of the greatest children's films of all time. What was the book?
   The Wonderful Wizard of Oz (but you can have a point for The Wizard of Oz).

5. We've all heard of Rudolph the red-nosed reindeer, but in the poem A Visit from St Nicholas, more often known by its first line 'Twas the night before Christmas, Santa had eight other reindeer. Can you name them?
   Dasher, Dancer, Prancer, Vixen, Comet, Cupid, Donner and Blitzen. Donner and Blitzen are the German words for thunder and lightning, which are fine names for flying reindeer, however they only became known by these names more than 100 years after Santa's reindeers were originally named. So, if you called them by the earlier names of Dunder, Donder, Blixem or Blixen, then give yourself an extra imaginary point!

6. The Adventure of the Blue Carbuncle was a Christmas themed Sherlock Holmes Mystery. Can you name Sherlock's medically trained partner?
Doctor Watson.

7. For a Sherlock Holmes bonus, who wrote the original books? Arthur C. Clarke, Arthur Conan Doyle, or Robert Louis Stevenson?
The books were written by Scottish author *Arthur Conan Doyle*. Conan Doyle was a huge fan of mystical and unexplained phenomenon, and apparently believed that a famous 1917 picture showing a young girl playing with fairies was real. The pictures were unfortunately fake.

8. Which of these three Christmas movies isn't based on a book? The Polar Express, Elf, or How the Grinch Stole Christmas?
Elf. The story was written for the big screen by David Berenbaum. The Polar Express and How the Grinch Stole Christmas are based on stories by Chris Van Allsburg and Dr. Seuss respectively.

Answers – Eat, Drink & Be Merry: The Quiz

1. What Christmas drink often involves spirits, such as rum or brandy being added to a milky drink?
   Eggnog. Usually made with milk or cream, and added whipped eggs then topped with spices such as cinnamon or nutmeg. We have no idea of the true origin, but hats off to whoever decided alcohol and eggs were a good mix!

2. What is the name of the traditional Italian Christmas bread loaf?
   Panettone. This light cake is a popular alternative to Christmas Cake in a growing number of countries worldwide.

3. What do Norwegians call the warmed wine they drink at Christmas time? Gløgg, Gøøgle, or Grølsch?
   It's *Gløgg!* Hot wine is popular in many places, especially countries that are a bit chillier, and is known by various names such as Glögi in Finland, Glühwein in Germany, and Mulled Wine in English speaking countries.

4. Puto Bumbong is a purple sticky rice cake, eaten at Christmas in which country? The Philippines, Ghana, or Peru?
   The Philippines. The colour comes from the purple yam.

5. Szaloncukor is popular in Hungary at Christmas – but what is it? A sausage, a drink, or a sweet?
   It's a *sweet* – usually a fondant covered in chocolate.

6. In Britain, pig's head smothered in mustard used to be a popular Christmas dish. True or False?
   It's *True*. So if you want a 'traditional' Christmas, you now know what to eat!

7. What is Stollen? A Finnish name for Santa, a German fruit cake, or a word we've just made up?
   It's a *German fruit cake*, and very lovely it is too!

8. Poor turkeys don't do well out of Christmas, but it used to be worse for them. In the 18th Century, not only were tens of thousands eaten each year in London, but they had to walk there from the turkey farms in Norfolk – a distance of up to 100 miles. What did they wear to help them during the journey?
   Boots! It was so far that they'd often damage their feet on the way, so their feet were dipped in tar, which provided a protective 'boot'.

Answers – Sing-a-long-a-Christmas-quiz

1. What's the worldwide biggest selling Christmas song of all time? White Christmas, All I Want for Christmas Is You, or Last Christmas?
   White Christmas, written by Irving Berlin and sung by Bing Crosby in the 1940s has sold an estimated 50 million copies! An honourable mention goes to Do They Know It's Christmas, the charity single by Band Aid which was the UK's biggest selling single when it was released.

2. Which decidedly odd pairing dueted on a version of Little Drummer Boy in 1977?
   David Bowie and Bing Crosby. Bowie had an early hit with a song called the Laughing Gnome, and later spent years recording as a character called Ziggy Stardust. Yet even by his standards, this is impressively odd. The unusual collaboration was recorded for Bing Crosby's 1977 TV Christmas Special. Sadly Bing passed away before the show was aired.

3. What colourful Christmas song did Elvis make famous?
   Blue Christmas.

4. Which ex-Beatle sang Happy Xmas (War Is Over)? And for a bonus point, what was the name of the 1979 Christmas song by another ex-Beatle?
   John Lennon sang Happy Xmas (War Is Over) in 1971 (although a dispute over publishing rights meant it wasn't released in the UK till Xmas 1972), while Paul McCartney sang *Wonderful Christmastime* in 1979.

5. Nat King Cole sings the line "Chestnuts roasting on an open fire" in which Christmas song? The clue was in the question – it's actually called *The Christmas Song!*

6. She & Him released an entire album of Christmas tunes in 2011 called "A Very She & Him Christmas". One half of the band is known for her comedy show New Girl – who is 'She'?
   Zooey Deschanel. The 'Him' is M. Ward, and as far as we know he doesn't star in any comedy shows.

7. Jimmy Boyd was the boy who saw "...Mommy Kissing Santa Claus" in the 1950s, but how old was the 'boy' when he recorded the song? 8, 13, or 25?
   He was 13, and as with another famous Christmas song (the one about a red nosed reindeer), this was written for an ad campaign. The song was commissioned by a US department store, Saks Fifth Avenue, to promote a Christmas card.

8. Which singer, who died on Christmas Day 2006, famously sang "Get Up"?
   James Brown. In a confusing twist another of his greatest hits, The Boss, asked us to "Get down". Perhaps what he really wanted was for us all to bounce up and down all day like crazy Kangaroos?!

9. Christmas songs are usually associated with pop acts, but which alternative rock band released a yearly Christmas song? Coldplay, Radiohead or The Killers?
   The Killers have released numerous Christmas songs to raise money for the charity Project Red, which supports the Global Fund to Fight AIDS, Tuberculosis and Malaria.

10. Which family group released a version of 'Santa Claus is Coming to Town' in 1970? The Jackson 5 or The Osmonds?
    The Jackson 5. They released an entire Christmas album that year, and Santa Claus is Coming to Town was the first single.

11. And for your bonus - the notes below are a slightly wonky version of *Rudolph the Red Nosed Reindeer*.

Answers – The Search is on for Christmas

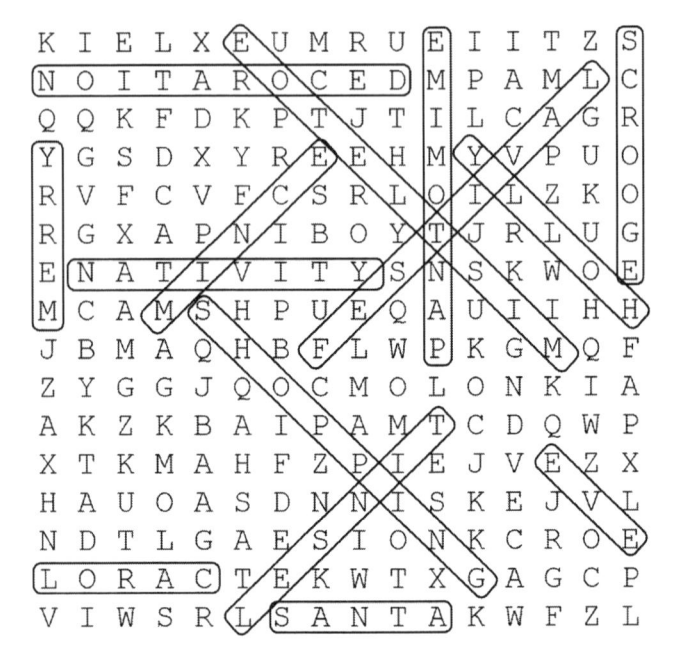

```
K I E L X E U M R U E I I T Z S
N O I T A R O C E D M P A M L C
Q Q K F D K P T J T I L C A G R
Y G S D X Y R E H M Y V P U O
R V F C V F C S R L O I Z K O
R G X A P N I B O Y T J R L U G
E N A T I V I T Y S N S K W O E
M C A M S H P U E Q A U I I H H
J B M A Q H B F L W P K G M Q F
Z Y G G J Q O C M O L O N K I A
A K Z K B A I P A M T C D Q W P
X T K M A H F Z P I E J V E Z X
H A U O A S D N N I S K E J V L
N D T L G A E S I O N K C R O E
L O R A C T E K W T X G A G C P
V I W S R L S A N T A K W F Z L
```

Answers – 12 Days of Wordsearch

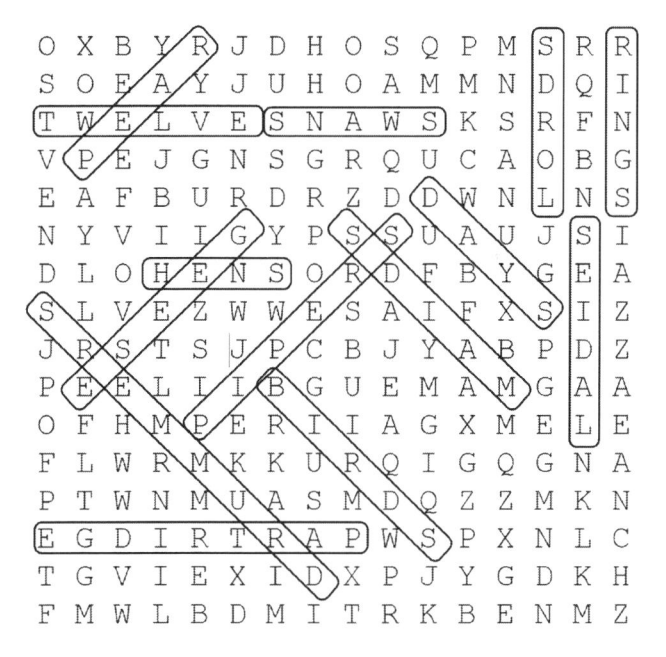

```
O X B Y R J D H O S Q P M S R R
S O E A Y J U H O A M M N D Q I
T W E L V E S N A W S K S R F N
V P E J G N S G R Q U C A O B G
E A F B U R D R Z D D W N L N S
N Y V I I G Y P S S U A U J S I
D L O H E N S O R D F B Y G E A
S L V E Z W W E S A I F X S I Z
J R S T S J P C B J Y A B P D Z
P E E L L I B G U E M A M G A A
O F H M P E R I I A G X M E L E
F L W R M K K U R Q I G Q G N A
P T W N M U A S M D Q Z Z M K N
E G D I R T R A P W S P X N L C
T G V I E X I D X P J Y G D K H
F M W L B D M I T R K B E N M Z
```

Answers – It's a Wonderful Wordsearch!

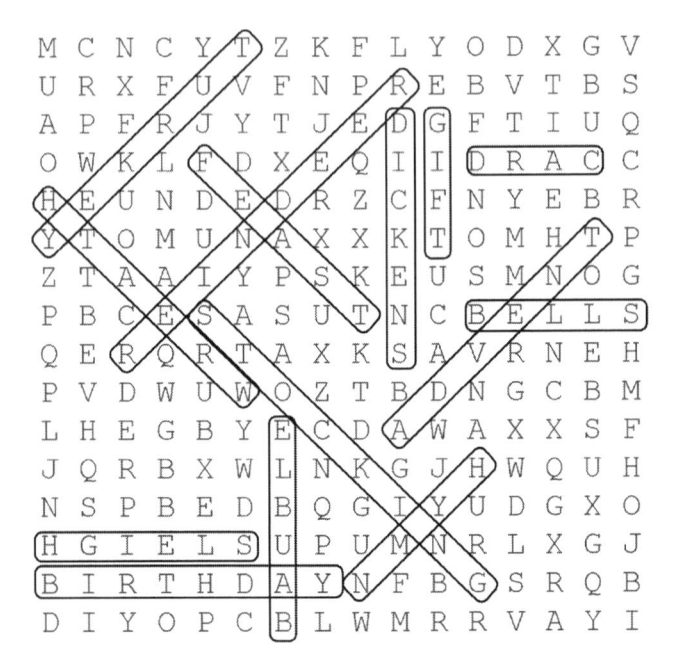

```
M C N C Y T Z K F L Y O D X G V
U R X F U V F N P R E B V T B S
A P F R J Y T J E D G F T I U Q
O W K L F D X E Q I I D R A C C
H E U N D E R Z C F N Y E B R
Y T O M U N A X X K T O M H T P
Z T A A I Y P S K E U S M N O G
P B C E S A S U T N C B E L L S
Q E R Q R T A X K S A V R N E H
P V D W U W O Z T B D N G C B M
L H E G B Y E C D A W A X X S F
J Q R B X W L N K G J H W Q U H
N S P B E D B Q G I Y U D G X O
H G I E L S U P U M N R L X G J
B I R T H D A Y N F B G S R Q B
D I Y O P C B L W M R R V A Y I
```

Answers - Spot the difference

Star upside down, missing button on gingerbread man, missing glove on gingerbread man, missing parachute line, missing berry on snowman's hat, missing berry on snowman's smile, stripes on gift reversed, missing leg on robin, extra snowman button, different label on wine.

Answers - Santa Jigsaw

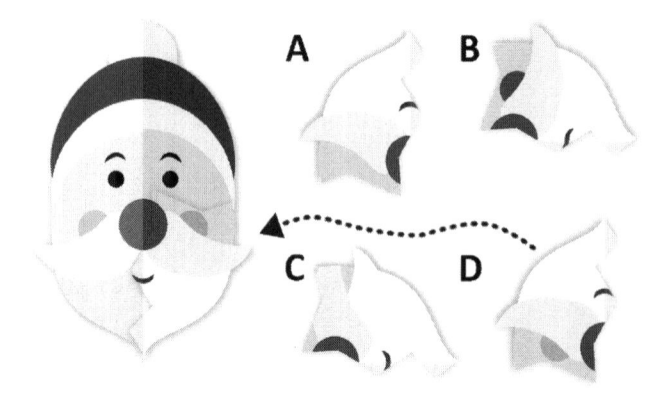

Answers –
Hcrismtsa All lmdex Pu*

1. Jingle All the Way

2. The Santa Clause

3. Elf

4. The Nightmare Before Christmas

5. Holiday Inn

6. Christmas with the Kranks

7. It's a Very Merry Muppet Christmas

8. Four Christmases

9. The Family Stone

10. Scrooged

*Christmas All Mixed Up

Answers – Cleverer than a Santa with two brains?

Which Elf will arrive on December 22nd? *Chipper*

Who will travel by reindeer? *Buddy*

Who will make the Teddy Bear? *Chipper*

	20th	21st	22nd	23rd	24th	Train Set	Toy Soldier	Yoyo	Teddy Bear	Jigsaw	Sleigh	Reindeer	Skis	Snowmobile	Dog Sled
Chipper	✗	✗	✓	✗	✗	✗	✗	✗	✓	✗	✗	✗	✓	✗	✗
Sugarplum	✗	✓	✗	✗	✗	✗	✗	✗	✗	✓	✗	✗	✗	✗	✓
Tootsie	✗	✗	✗	✓	✗	✗	✓	✗	✗	✗	✗	✗	✗	✓	✗
Buddy	✓	✗	✗	✗	✗	✗	✗	✓	✗	✗	✗	✓	✗	✗	✗
Pixie	✗	✗	✗	✗	✓	✓	✗	✗	✗	✗	✓	✗	✗	✗	✗
Sleigh	✗	✗	✗	✗	✓	✓	✗	✗	✗	✗					
Reindeer	✓	✗	✗	✗	✗	✗	✗	✓	✗	✗					
Skis	✗	✗	✓	✗	✗	✗	✗	✗	✓	✗					
Snowmobile	✗	✗	✗	✓	✗	✗	✓	✗	✗	✗					
Dog Sled	✗	✓	✗	✗	✗	✗	✗	✗	✗	✓					
Train Set	✗	✗	✗	✗	✓										
Toy Soldier	✗	✗	✗	✓	✗										
Yoyo	✓	✗	✗	✗	✗										
Teddy Bear	✗	✗	✓	✗	✗										
Jigsaw	✗	✓	✗	✗	✗										

Printed in Great Britain
by Amazon.co.uk, Ltd.,
Marston Gate.